IS

TURKEY

Travel Guide Book

A Comprehensive 5-Day Travel Guide to Istanbul,
Turkey & Unforgettable Turkish Travel

♦ Travel Guides to Europe Series ♦

Passport to European Travel Guides

☙

Eye on Life Publications

Istanbul, Turkey Travel Guide Book
Copyright © 2015 Passport to European Travel Guides

ISBN 10: 1519149174
ISBN 13: 978-1519149176

~

Other Travel Guide Books by Passport to European Travel Guides

Top 10 Travel Guide to Italy

Florence, Italy

Rome, Italy

Venice, Italy

Naples & the Amalfi Coast, Italy

Paris, France

Provence & the French Riviera, France

Top 10 Travel Guide to France

London, England

Barcelona, Spain

Amsterdam, Netherlands

Santorini, Greece

Greece & the Greek Islands

Berlin, Germany

Munich, Germany

Vienna, Austria

Budapest, Hungary

Prague, Czech Republic

Brussels, Belgium

"If one had but a single glance to give the world, one should gaze on Istanbul."—Alphonse de Lamartine

Table of Contents

• Map of Istanbul, Turkey •

• Introduction •

Istanbul, Turkey. Regarded as the largest city in the country, Istanbul is not only considered the historical, cultural and financial heart of Turkey, but it's also a transcontinental city of **Eurasia** that encompasses both Europe and Asia.

Istanbul is indeed the spot where the **East meets the West**, while at the same time straddling both the **ancient and modern worlds**. And as if that's not enough, this city also boasts being the only one to have served as the capital of both the consecutive Christian and Islamic empires, a role that actually shaped the region's history for more than nearly 2,500 years.

Today, this historic city is a bustling force **of spectacular attractions.**

In this 5-day guide to Istanbul, Turkey, you'll get the sharpest recommendations and **tips** to best prepare you with everything you need to know in order to have a most successful and memorable Turkish experience!

Read over the insider tips carefully and familiarize yourself with the information so you can pack and prepare accordingly. Every traveler is different, so we've included a variety of information and recommendations to suit all interests. You can plan according to our **detailed 5-day itinerary** or you can mix it up and **mix and match the activities** and scheduling. We invite you to do whatever works for the enjoyment of your trip!

Enjoy!

The Passport to European Travel Guides Team

• City Snapshot •

Language: Turkish
Local Airports:
Atatürk International Airport
Sabiha Gökçen International Airport

Currency: Turkish Lira (₺)
Country Code: 90
Emergencies: Dial 112

• Before You Go... •

✓ Have a Passport

If you don't already have one, you'll need to apply for a passport in your home country a good two months before you intend to travel, to avoid cutting it too close. **You'll need to find a local passport agency**, complete an application, take fresh photos of yourself, have at least one form of ID and pay an application fee. **If you're in a hurry**, you can usually expedite the application for a 2-3 week turnaround at an additional cost.

✓ Need a Visa?

American citizens wanting to travel to Turkey on U.S. passports must have a visa. Not a traditional visa, but an electronic visa (e-Visa). Most European travelers do not need a visa unless they plan to stay in Turkey for more than 90 days. If you're unsure whether or not you need a visa, check the current list on the **Republic of Turkey's** website:
http://www.mfa.gov.tr/visa-information-for-foreigners.en.mfa

In order to obtain your e-Visa, you simply log on to the Republic of Turkey's website, complete the forms, make an online payment and then download your e-Visa:
http://www.evisa.gov.tr

Note: e-Visas are valid for **tourism and short stays** only. They are not valid for working or going to school in Turkey.

The US State Department provides a wealth of country-specific information for American travelers, including **travel alerts and warnings**, the location of the **US embassy in each country**, and of course, **whether or not you need a visa** to travel there!
http://travel.state.gov/content/passports/english/country.html

✓ Healthcare

Most people neglect this but it's important to keep in mind when traveling to any foreign country. It's wise to consult with your doctor about your travel plans and ensure routine immunizations are current. You want to protect against things like influenza, polio, chickenpox, mumps, measles, etc. **Turkey is no exception**.

It's always a good idea to have traveler's insurance so you know you're covered. There are **public and private healthcare** options in Turkey. You will need to pay doctors or nurses in cash, and private hospitals provide good care but tend to be very expensive. For minor injuries such as cuts and scrapes, bring along your own first-aid kit. Should you have a true life-threatening emergency, your hotel should be able to direct you to the nearest health center (*sağulık ocağuı* in Turkish). **Note:** Medical personnel in health centers typically speak Turkish only. Your insurance carrier may also be able to provide travel assistance so it's a good idea to contact them before you go.

✓ Set the Date

For the best experience, we recommend visiting Istanbul during the summer months **June, July and August**. It is the high season for tourism (meaning higher prices), but that's when most fun festivals and various other events take place.

While it can get quite steamy in various parts of Turkey this time of year, **Istanbul typically averages** daily temperatures up to 80°F; warm, but not unbearable.

For better rates, always try to book your flights and hotel rooms as far in advance as possible.

✓ Pack

When traveling to Istanbul, keep in mind that it is a **Muslim country** and many of the places people usually visit are mosques. So if you are a woman, be sure to pack respectful clothes and always wear a scarf. Also, pack **comfortable walking shoes.**

• **Travelers from outside Europe** will need to bring along a **universal electrical plug converter** that can work for both lower and higher voltages. This way you'll be able to plug in your cell phones, tablets, curling irons, etc., during the trip.

• **Although English** is spoken around the tourist areas, **less than 20%** of the Turkish population actually speaks

English. (Some speak German and French.) Bring a **Turkish phrase book** along with you so you can greet appropriately and ask common questions.

• If you're visiting **Istanbul in the summer**, don't forget **a hat and sunscreen**. And no matter the time of year, **bring an umbrella and raincoat.** Showers and drizzles can often interrupt sightseeing.

• Be sure to **leave expensive jewels and high-priced electronics at home**. Like most major cities and tourist attractions, thieves and pickpockets can be anywhere. Avoid making yourself a target.

• A simple **first aid kit** is always a good idea to have in your luggage, just in case.

• **Hand sanitizer** is always great to have along with you when traveling.

• **Medication.** Don't forget to have enough for the duration of your trip. It's also helpful to have a **note from your physician** in case you're questioned for carrying a certain quantity.

• You can bring one or two **reusable shopping bags** for bringing souvenirs home.

• **Take pictures of your travel documents and your passport** and email them to yourself before your trip. This can help in the unfortunate event they are lost or stolen.

• **Pack well,** but be sure to leave room for souvenirs!

✓ Phone Home

Before leaving for Istanbul, check out your cell phone company's international calling and texting plans. You can also **keep in touch via Skype, Google Talk**, or any other free Internet communications service; or purchase a phone card (telekart) once you land at the airport in Turkey. For longer stays, a **Turkish SIM card** or a **prepaid phone** is also a good option.

✓ Currency Exchange

The local currency in Turkey is the **Turkish lira**, so you'll need to exchange your USD ($) for TL ("). For better exchange rates, we recommend buying your Turkish lira in Turkey rather than your home country.

✓ Contact Your Embassy

In the unfortunate event that you should lose your passport or be victimized while away, **your country's embassy** will be able to help you. Be sure to give your itinerary and contact information to a **close friend or family member**, then also contact your embassy with your emergency contact information before you leave.

✓ Your Mail

Ask a neighbor to **check your mailbox** while you're away or visit your local post office and request a hold. **Overflowing mailboxes** are a dead giveaway that no one's home.

• Getting in the Mood •

Here are a few great books and films **about or set in Istanbul** that we recommend you watch in preparation for your trip to this historic city!

What to Read:

• **Don't miss The Bastard of Istanbul** by Elif Shafak, one of Turkey's most celebrated writers. Set against the backdrop of the country's violent history, two families—one Turkish, one Armenian American—struggle to reconcile their individual identities. Great reading!

• **For a beautifully** intimate and moving portrait of Istanbul from a loyal, Nobel Prize-winning Turkish native, check out, **Istanbul: Memories and the City** by Orhan Pamuk.

• **And your preparation** for visiting Istanbul won't be complete without reading, **A Mind at Peace** by Ahmet Hamdi Tanpinar! The authentic characters in this lyrically dramatic homage to Istanbul leap right off the page and into your heart.

What to Watch:

• **Our top recommendation** is definitely 2002's **Distant**, directed by Nuri Bilge Ceylan! Considered one of the best Turkish films of all time, this compelling and dramatic story is sure to move you in unexpected ways.

• **Haven't seen Sean Connery** in 1963's **From Russia With Love?** Follow James Bond to Istanbul and see what happens!

• **And you simply must** check out, **The International (2009).** Great performances from Clive Owen and Naomi Watts with fabulous scenes shot in Istanbul!

• Local Tourist Information •

Upon your arrival at either Atatürk International Airport or Sabiha Gökçen International Airport, you will find a tourist information office + plenty of kiosks where you can **pick up brochures, maps** and other helpful information.

Istanbul also has several official **tourist information offices** (In Turkish: Turist Danışma Ofisi) throughout the European side of the city. All have English-speaking agents ready to be of service. Here's the most current list of office locations, phone numbers and hours of operation:

• **Atatürk Havalimanı**
Location: Atatürk Airport — Yeşilköy, 34149, İstanbul, Turkey
Hours: 8:00am - 11:00 pm — 7 days a week
Tel: +90 212 465 31 51 | | +90 212 465 35 47

• **Taksim Hilton Otel**
Location: Hilton Hotel — Elmadağ / Taksim (Hilton Hotel entrances)
Hours: 8:30am to 4:45pm, closed on Sundays
Tel: +90 212 233 05 92

• **Sultanahmet**
Location: At Meydanı — Sultanahmet
Hours: 9:00 am - 5:00pm — 7 days a week

Tel: +90 212 518 18 02

• **Karaköy**
Location: Karaköy Limanı – Karaköy (inside cruise ship terminal)
Hours: Call for current hours
Tel.: +90 212 249 57 76

• **Sirkeci**
Location: Sirkeci Tren İstasyonu – Sirkeci Train Station
Hours: 9:00am - 5:00pm — 7 days a week
Tel: +90 212 511 58 88

• **Beyazıt**
Location: Beyazıt Meydanı –Beyazıt square
Hours: 8:30am - 6:00pm — 7 days a week
Tel: +90 212 522 49 02

You can also purchase **Istanbul Tourist Passes** from www.istanbultouristpass.com! There are a variety of passes based on what you'd like to do in the city — visit museums, take boat tours, hire guides, etc. Check out their website for the most current options and pricing information.

• About the Airports •

Istanbul Atatürk International Airport
Address: Yeşilköy, 34149, İstanbul, Turkey
Tel: +90 212 463 3000
Website: http://www.ataturkairport.com/en-EN/Pages/Main.aspx

This is Turkey's largest airport and Istanbul's main one, located 15 miles west of the city center.

Sabiha Gökçen International Airport
Address: Sanayi Mh, 34906, İstanbul, Turkey
Tel: +90 216 588 8000
Website: http://www.sabihagokcen.aero/homepage

This smaller airport is 22 miles southeast of the city center, on the Asian side of Istanbul. This one serves many budget airlines and domestic flights.

• How Long is the Flight? •

- **From New York** to Istanbul = approx. 10.5 hours

- **From Chicago** to Istanbul = approx. 11.5 hours

- **From Los Angeles** to Istanbul = approx. 13.5 hours

- **From Miami** to Istanbul = approx. 15 hours

- **From London** to Istanbul = approx. 4 hours

- **From Sydney** to Istanbul = approx. 20.5 hours

- **From Cape Town** to Istanbul = approx. 13 hours

• Overview of Istanbul •

Istanbul is located in the northwest of Turkey, where the Bosphorus strait connects the Sea of Marmara to the Black Sea and divides the land into the Thracian side (European) and the Anatolian side (Asian).

With a population of approximately 12-19 million, Istanbul is a large city, divided into at least 39 districts that include **Karaköy**, **New City**, **Bosphorus** and **Golden Horn**, as well as the **Princes' Island** and the **Old City of Istanbul, Sultanahmet**.

Not only is Istanbul Turkey's economic, cultural and historical heart, but the city is in fact so populated that it stands as **one of the largest**, not just in Europe, but in the world. And it's incidentally also well known for having some of the most **friendly and welcoming** residents you can find anywhere.

Modern-day Istanbul may surprise you. Having emerged in recent years as the land of the cool and trendy, many areas have been transformed by stylish restaurants and shops, attractive boutique hotels and inns, and super chic nightclubs. We promise you — **a great time awaits you in Istanbul.** Read on!

• Insider Tips for Tourists •

When traveling to a new place it's always great to get a good feel for what it will be like to actually *be* there. So we've got some **useful tips for newbies** to Turkey.

• Always **keep your phrasebook handy**. Learning common greetings, goodbyes, and phrases like: "How much is this?" or "Where is the restroom?" (in Turkish and/or Arabic) can definitely make things smoother for you while in Istanbul.

• While **navigating the bustling city** of Istanbul's totally doable for foreigners, we still recommend you hire **a qualified tour guide** in this city. You're much more likely to **get the most** out of your trip and, in many cases, **save yourself time and money**. There are many options and specialties, depending on your interests: http://www.tripadvisor.com/Travel-g293969-c18975/Turkey:Tour.Guides.In.Turkey.html

• To avoid spending much of your time in Istanbul **waiting in traffic jams**, we recommend arranging for private tour buses, taxis, vans or mini-buses for larger parties. See our **upcoming recommendations** for the best companies.

• Most of the **popular attractions in Istanbul** are close to one another, within walking distance in many cases, so it's good to be prepared for **lots of walking**.

• Thieves and pickpockets abound in **tourist areas**. Be mindful of con men and women and smart thieves who may **approach you** as a distraction. **Leave your valuables** at home and we don't advise carrying an excess amount of cash. If you're lost, ask for help yourself. Be cautious of anyone who approaches you offering his or her help.

• **Be careful what you photograph** in Istanbul. **Fully covered women** do not wish to be photographed and it is impolite to do so without her permission. You'll see a picture of a crossed out camera in museums where cameras are not allowed. It is also illegal to photograph government buildings, police, military, etc.

• Be aware that **Istanbul, Turkey is a very humble city**. A tourist or visitor's goal is to experience the culture; not expect to find extravagant Italian restaurants and the like as you may have back home.

Etiquette

Turkish people are **modern people** who love to keep their **traditions alive**. Etiquette is very important to learn so you can **blend well** and avoid awkward situations or causing offense in this culture.

• Turks are very enthusiastic greeters! When **meeting or greeting** Turkish people, shake hands with everyone present: men, women and children

• Try not to stand with your **hands on your hips** when talking to others

• Placing your **thumb between your index and middle** fingers is the equivalent of flipping someone off with the middle finger in the United States

• Don't raise the sole of your foot toward anyone, it's considered very rude. When sitting, be mindful to keep your feet flat on the ground

• In Turkey, **the thumbs up "OK" gesture** means that someone is homosexual. It's best to avoid using the thumbs up sign while you're there

• **When finished with meals**, place your silverware side-by-side on your plate when you're done

• Smoking has been banned in public places, however don't be surprised to find many **people still smoking during meals** in certain places. You probably shouldn't bother requesting they stop

Time Zone

The time difference between **New York and Istanbul is 7 hours**. Istanbul is ahead on the clock. (When it's 8AM in New York, it's 3PM in Istanbul).

The time difference between **London and Istanbul is 2 hours**. Istanbul is ahead on the clock. (8AM in London is 10AM in Istanbul).

The time difference between **Sydney, Australia and Istanbul is 7 hours**. Sidney is ahead on the clock. (When it's 8AM in Istanbul, it's 3PM in Sidney).

Daylight Savings Time: Turkish clocks are turned ahead one hour on the last Sunday in March, and turned back one hour on the last Sunday in October.

The format for abbreviating dates in Europe is different from the US. They use: **day/month/year**. So for example, August 23, 2019 is written in Europe as 23 August 2019, or 23/8/19.

Saving Time & Money

• Our biggest piece of advice to help you **save both time and money** is to grab yourself a nicely detailed map of the city. Walking shorter distances cuts way down on transportation expenses

• Definitely grab an **Istanbul Tourist Pass** as previously mentioned. If you're only spending a week in Istanbul, it's best to have your itinerary largely mapped out beforehand

• For hotel accommodations, if you're **on a tight budget,** we recommended staying at a 3–star hotel (we have excellent budget recommendations ahead). **The view from your window** may not be so great, but you want to enjoy your experience traipsing around Istanbul, right? Not cooped up in your hotel room staring at the view. Staying in a **3-star hotel** can typically cost under $100 USD per night

• Do not forget to **notify your banks and credit card companies** about your travel plans to avoid having your overseas charges blocked as fraud protection

• Try to avoid doing too much **shopping and dining in tourist areas** if you're on a budget. If you venture just a few streets, you can **eat where the locals do**...and pay lower prices.

Tipping

Tips, or as they call them in Turkey, *bahşiş,* are **usually modest**. You may notice a big difference between the amounts you to tip in the United States verses the amounts in Istanbul.

• **Tip in cash**. You won't likely be able to include gratuity on your credit card. And for smaller tips, be sure to use the local currency, Turkish lira, not U.S dollars

• **Taxi drivers** are not usually tipped in Turkey, but it's customary to **round your fare up** to the next lira. So for example, if your fare is 6.5 liras, you may round it up to 7 liras

• At the **airports, bus and train stations, professional porters** work under official tariff. In case you don't see it prominently posted, just tip 2-3 Turkish liras per bag. If it's less than the authorized tariff, the porter will let you know

• It's appropriate to tip **hotel porters** anywhere from 2-4 Turkish liras per bag

• For **housekeeping staff** in moderately-priced hotels, you can tip them from 5-7 liras per day

• When eating in **inexpensive restaurants,** tip about 5% of the bill. In **luxury restaurants,** tip 10-15%

• Be sure to tip **tour guides and drivers** on organized tours as a group. It's appropriate to tip them 20-30 liras per day (about $10-$15 US)

• Should you decide to visit a **Turkish bath** (called Hamam in Turkey) — and we thoroughly recommend that you do — leave a 15% tip

When You Have to Go

Public restrooms in Turkey are marked with either: "**WC**," "**Tuvalet**," or "**00**". *Bay* is for male and *Bayan* is for female.

All mosques have toilets that you can use for free.

Additionally, it's very likely you'll run into **Turkish-style toilets** a.k.a. old-fashioned "squat toilets." Be sure to **step as far away** as you can when you flush to avoid having water splash your shoes or clothes.

Taxes

A standard 18% **Value Added Tax** (VAT) is included in the price of just about every purchase. VAT is a standard consumption tax throughout the European Union.

Visitors can benefit from **Duty Free or Tax Free** shopping in Turkey via refund for VAT. Great news, right?

Just look for a **"Tax Free" logo**, spend more than 108 Turkish lira + VAT in a day, and ask the shop or store to prepare a **Global Refund Cheque** (GRC) when paying for your purchases. Then pay a visit to the Customs Office in the Atatürk International Airport of Istanbul the day you leave Turkey. Show them the Global Refund Cheques, your receipts and passport. Once they stamp your GRC, you can then retrieve your money in any Cash Refund Office in the world. **Be sure to take care of this** before checking your luggage.

Turkish restaurants and hotels typically **include taxes in their prices**, but if you notice anything excessive or abnormal, just ask for the manager.

Phone Calls

The country code for Turkey is 90. There are 3 major "GSM Operators" in Turkey:

Turkcell: www.turkcell.com.tr

Vodafone: www.vodafone.com.tr

Avea: www.avea.com.tr

If you don't have an **international roaming plan** with your current carrier, check their rates before you go.

You can buy a **prepaid SIM card** as soon as you arrive at the airport in Istanbul. You would then have a **Turkish phone number** and incoming calls are free in Turkey, so others would be able to reach you without charge. **Check with your carrier** to make sure your cell phone is **compatible** with other carrier SIM cards; if it's not, you have the option of **renting a cell phone** from one of the above GSM operators for the duration of your stay.

To phone the US from Turkey dial: 00 + 1 + the area code and phone number

To phone Turkey from the United States dial: 011 + 90 + area code and phone number

Electricity

Turkey operates on 220 volts, 50 Hz, with round-prong **European-style socket plugs**, but some hotels (mostly four- and five-star hotels) can provide North American-style converters for 120 volts, 60 Hz.

It's always a good idea to buy an **adapter and converter** at the airport before you leave so you can **plug your electronics into the wall sockets** once you get to Istanbul. Laptop computers and digital cameras usually don't need convertors, just adapters, unlike hair dryers, traveling irons, etc.

In Emergencies

911 won't work in Turkey, so in emergencies, use any of these numbers:

For Medical Emergency/**Ambulance**: Dial 112
For **Fire**: Dial 110
To contact the **police**: Dial 155
To contact the **coastguard**: Dial: 158
In case of a **missing child** or in need of **Women's Helpline**: Dial 183

Turkish Phrases for Emergencies:

Accident	Kaza
Emergency	Acil / ilk yardım

Fire	Yangın
Help me	Yardım edin, yardım lütfen
Hospital	Hastane
Medicine	İlaç
Faint	Bayılma
I have had an accident	Kaza yaptım
Injured	Yaralıyım
Unconscious	Bilinç kaybı
Bleeding	Kanama
Heart attack	Kalp krizi
Stroke	Felç / inme / darbe
Drowning	Boğulma
Burn	Yanma / yanık
Very sick	Çok hasta
In labour / having contractions	Kasılma / gerilme
Need a doctor	Doktor çağırın / doktora ihtiyaç var
Need an ambulance	Ambulans çağırın, ambulansa ihtiyaç var

The house is on fire	Ev yanıyor / evde yangın var
The car is on fire	Araba yanıyor
I am being burgled	Soyuldum
Someone is in the house	Evde biri var / Evde hırsız olabilir

Holidays

Holiday	Date
New Year's Day	01 January
Milad-un-Nabi (Birthday of Prophet Mohammed)	Muslim Calendar
Republic Day	26 January
Holi	06 March
Ram Navmi	28 March
Labour and Solidarity Day	01 May
Idu'l Fitr	Muslim Calendar
Independence Day	15 August
Janmashtami	The 8th day of the dark fortnight of the month of Bhadrapada
Id-ul-Zuha (Bakrid)	Muslim Calendar
Mahatma Gandhi's Birthday	02 October
Dussehra	22 October
Muharram	Muslim Calendar

Republic Day of Turkey	29 October
Diwali	11 November
Guru Nanak's Birthday	25 November
Milad-un-Nabi	24 December
Christmas	25 December

Hours of Operation

• **Istanbul's Metro and tram system** runs from **6 am to midnight**

• **Most business hours** are between **8:30am and 6:00pm; Lunch hours** are between **noon and 1:30pm**

• **Large shopping centers** typically stay open **until 9:00pm**

• **Some restaurants** stay open 24 hours a day

• **Museums in Istanbul** are open 6 days a week, between **9:30am and 5:00pm**

Here's a quick look at the opening hours of some of the most popular spots to visit while in Istanbul:

• **Blue Mosque** (Sultanahmet Camii)

<u>Open</u>: Daily from 9:00am till dusk

Closed: 30 mins before until 30 mins after prayer time, 2 hours during Friday noon prayer

• **Archaeological Museum** (Arkeoloji Müzeleri)

Open: Daily from 9:00am – 5:00pm, no entrance after 4:00pm

Closed: Mondays, and until 12:00 noon on the first day of religious holidays

• **Dolmabahçe Palace** (Dolmabahçe Sarayı)

Open: Daily from 9:00am – 4:00pm

Closed: Mondays, Thursdays, January 1st, and the first days of religious holidays

• **Egyptian or Spice Bazaar** (Mısır Çarşısı)

Open: Daily from 8:00am – 7:00pm

Closed: Sundays, October 29th and the full duration of religious holidays

• **Süleymaniye Mosque** (Süleymaniye Camii)

Open: Daily from 9:00pm – 5:30pm

Closed: During prayer time

• **Topkapi Palace** (Topkapı Sarayı)

Open: Daily from 9:00am – 5:00pm

Closed: Tuesdays, and until 12:00 noon on the first day of religious holidays

List of official and religious days off in Istanbul:

• New Year's Day, 1 January
• The Feast of Ramadan, (3.5 days)
• The Feast of Sacrifice, (4.5 days)
• National Sovereignty, Commemoration of Atatürk, Youth and Sports Day, 19 May
• Republic Day, 29 October
• Victory Day, 30 August

Money

US dollars can still be used **for certain expenses** like your hotel room or car rental, but you'll need **Turkish lira** to tip waiters or to pay for public transportation.

Also, large Turkish lira bills may be refused for small payments, so it's best to exchange for **smaller notes** and **coins** to shop, tip, and make minor purchases.

When using your credit or debit cards, if you're ever given the option to pay for something in Turkish lira or US dollars, **always choose Turkish lira** to avoid paying higher rates and fees.

Climate and Best Times to Travel

As we mentioned earlier, the summer months, **June, July and August** are typically the best times for visiting Istanbul. Really, anytime between **April and September** is best for **local weather and fun activities**.

The Istanbul Film Festival takes place for almost two full weeks **every other April**. The audience gets to watch contemporary Turkish films with **English subtitles**, and the screenings are held mainly in Beyoglu, Nisantasi or Kadikoy.

And then there's the **Istanbul Tulip Festival** in **April**, a time when parks all over the city erupt in living color!

The Istanbul Jazz Festival is also held in **June** and it mainly features classical music, whereas the Jazz Festival held the **first 2 weeks of July**, brings in the biggest names in jazz, from Turkey and around the world.

There's also the **Istanbul Biennial** and the **Istanbul Design Biennial** — held in odd number years and even number years respectively — showcasing innovative **artistic works** in venues around the city.

Transportation

Istanbul has one of the most **efficient and effective transport systems** in the world.

Rail transport—most trains travel through either the Sirkeci station or the Haydarpasa station, both serve the city 24/7.

Taxis—unlike many other European cities, cabs are very inexpensive in Istanbul.

Once you arrive, you'll notice that the light rail systems, consisting of the **metros and trams,** cover most parts of the city.

Although there are plenty of **airport buses, cabs and public transportation** options, in our opinion, a **private car service** is the way to go. It's relatively affordable in Istanbul and geared for your comfort. Someone will **await you at the airport** holding a sign with your name. We recommend **Efendi Travel** service. They also provide a variety of great city tours.

Efendi Travel
Address: Efendi Travel Akbiyik Cad. No: 30 Sultanahmet, Istanbul
Tel: +90 212 638 63 43
http://www.efenditravel.com/Istanbul-Airport-Transfers-efendimenu6876435897436-tid81

Driving

We don't recommend driving in Istanbul for tourists, unless you've previously driven in the city, you're very likely to end up lost and have a very hard time finding parking. However, if you should opt to rent a car, go with:

Europcar
Istanbul Taksim
Address: TOPCU CAD. N°:1 ELMADAG, 34437,
Istanbul
Tel: +90 212 254 7710
Code: ISTC01

• Tours •

Here are some of our **top recommendations** for a great time touring Istanbul!

Istanbul By Bike

You can join a half-day **Istanbul on Bike** tour (about 4 hours long) and cycle around the **Golden Horn** district (Haliç in Turkish) — the inlet of the Bosphorus strait that divides Istanbul into its two parts. This is basically a tour in two continents, Asia and Europe and the tour concludes with an amazing boat ride.

Meeting Point: In front of Kılıç Ali Paşa Mosque (nearby Tophane Tram Station).
Tel: +90 553 440 5544
http://www.istanbulonbike.com/bike-tours

Istanbul By Boat

Seeing Istanbul from the water will definitely be one of your holiday highlights. You'll discover the city is so incredibly beautiful! You can even tour some of the Islands of Greece!

There are **several great options** for boat tours, but from experience we recommend these two most. **Check their websites** for current tour packages and pricing:

Zoe Yacht Istanbul
Address: Kuruçeşme Cd, Beşiktaş, Istanbul
Tel: +90 532 200 7158
http://www.bosphorusyacht.com

Istanbul Boat Tours
Address: Akbıyık Cad. Bayramfırın Sok.no: 12, Sultanahmet, 34100, İstanbul
Tel: +90 552 559 2874
http://www.allbosphorusdinnercruises.com

Istanbul By Bus

A bus tour can also be nice, particularly if you're on a budget. It's one of the **least expensive yet insightful** ways to effortlessly tour Istanbul. Try any of these companies:

Plan Tours
Address: Cumhuriyet Cad. No: 83 D: 1, Elmadağ/Istanbul
Tel: +90 212 234 7777
http://www.plantours.com

Daily Istanbul Tours
Address: Divanyolu cad. Hacitahsin bey sok., No 5/A Sultanahmet, 34122, İstanbul
Tel: +90 535 587 6571

http://www.dailyistanbultours.com

Turkiye Tours
Address: Akşemseddin Mh., Hırka-i Şerif Cd, 34091,
Istanbul
Tel: +90 212 631 8262
http://www.turkiyetours.com

Istanbul By Minibus or Car

Efendi Travel is our best recommendation for mini-
bus or private car tour packages for small or large groups.

Efendi Travel
Address: Efendi Travel Akbiyik Cad. No: 30 Sul-
tanahmet, Istanbul
Tel: +90 212 638 63 43
http://www.efenditravel.com/Istanbul-Airport-
Transfers-efendimenu6876435897436-tid81

Try Special Interest and Walking Tours

For a more **specific and concentrated experience**, we
share our **top recommendations** for specialty tours
and exciting jaunts on foot.

Love food? Want to truly *taste* **Istanbul?** VIP Tourism offers a great time with **Street Food in Istanbul!**

Street Food in Istanbul
Tel: +90 212 368 48 54 or +90 212 368 47 52
http://www.viptourism.com/holiday/street-food-in-istanbul

For art enthusiasts, don't miss the 2-day **Byzantine Art** tour experience!

Istanbul Byzantine Treasures
Tel: +90 212 368 48 54 or +90 212 368 47 52
http://www.viptourism.com/holiday/istanbul-byzantine-treasures

Visit the **palaces of sultans** on the **Splendors of the Sultans** tour!

Splendors of the Sultans
Tel: +90 212 368 48 54 or +90 212 368 47 52
http://www.viptourism.com/holiday/splendors-of-the-sultans

And for those who may be curious about the **hidden passageways and dungeons** that lay beneath **Istanbul's modern-day veneers**, have we got an experience for you!

Underground Istanbul
Tel: +90 212 368 48 54 or +90 212 368 47 52
http://www.viptourism.com/holiday/underground-istanbul

For some of the most **beautiful walking tour experiences**, go with one of these, both offer unforgettable tours!

Istanbul Walks
Address: Küçük Ayasofya Mah. Sifahamami Sok.
No: 1 Kat:1 Sultanahmet, 34122, İstanbul
Tel: +90 212 516 6300
http://www.istanbulwalks.com

Walks in Istanbul
Address: Yerebatan Caddesi No: 9, 34122, Istanbul
Tel: +90 533 382 6047
http://www.walksinistanbul.com

• 5 Days in Istanbul! •

For most tourists traveling to Istanbul, especially if you're alone, we highly recommend that you **hire a professional and licensed tour guide** to help show you around the city. However, whether or not you decide to go it alone, we offer the following **5-day itinerary** that's sure to give you the best experience of the city. Always check websites for current hours of operations and visitor information as they often change.

Feel free to follow our schedule to the letter, or modify to your preferences. Either way — enjoy Istanbul!

• Day 1 •

Once you arrive in Istanbul (it's best to arrive in the morning) and get checked into your hotel room, try to relax a bit and get **refreshed and renewed** before heading out to explore.

Head over to one of Istanbul's star attractions: the **Hagia Sophia Museum** (Ayasofya in Turkish). Considered the **epitome of Byzantine architecture**, we think you'll be in sheer awe when you first walk through the door. It's open daily for touring but check the website for the most current visiting information.

If you arrive early enough and have the energy, you may be able to get to two more spots today. We recommend **voyaging underground** to see the Sunken Palace or **Basilica Cistern** (Yerebatan Sarayı), Istanbul's largest surviving Byzantine cisterns.

Next, walk over to the Sultan Ahmed Mosque or **Blue Mosque** (Sultanahmet Camii in Turkish). It's an active mosque and is closed to non-worshipers five times a day for about a half hour for prayer.

Conveniently, these three sites are very **close together**, so getting to them on your first day in Istanbul is totally doable.

After all the sightseeing, you'll likely be tired or jet lagged. Return to your hotel **for dinner** or have a quick dinner in the area you're staying in, then have a nice rest in preparation for tomorrow.

Location Information:

Hagia Sophia Museum
Address: Ayasofya Meydanı, Sultanahmet Fatih, 34410, Istanbul
Tel: +90 212 522 1750
http://ayasofyamuzesi.gov.tr/en

Basilica Cistern
Address: Imran Oktem Cad. No: 4 D:5 Sultanahmet, Fatih | Near St. Sophia, Istanbul
Tel: +90-212 522 12 59
http://yerebatan.com/homepage

The Blue Mosque
Address: Sultan Ahmet Mh., Torun Sk No:19, 34400 Istanbul
Tel: +90 212 458 4983
http://www.bluemosque.co

• Day 2 •

We're getting an early start today. Head over to the **Topkapı Palace Museum** first thing in the morning. As Istanbul's **number one tourist attraction**, it gets pretty crowded here! It's a massive complex that will leave you in total awe.

Next, head over to the **Istanbul Archaeology Museums** and enjoy this group of three archeological treasures!

Grab some lunch over at the nearby **Pizza de Lavia** before heading over to beautiful **Gülhane Park**, just a short walk from the museums and the perfect place for a soothing glass of Turkish tea!

Your next stop should be the **Galata Tower** (Galata Kulesi in Turkish), one of Istanbul's most striking landmarks. Climb to the top and check out that panoramic view of the city!

Afterwards you can arrange for a **guided tour** or stroll around and **shop for gifts and souvenirs**.

Ask a local for a great recommendation for dinner (always a good idea), then head back to your hotel and call it a night, or freshen up and get back out to experience **Istanbul's Nightlife**. Don't miss our recommended nightlife spots ahead!

Location Information:

Topkapı Palace Museum
Address: Gulhane Park, near Sultanahmet Square, Istanbul
Tel: +90 212 522 44 22
http://topkapisarayi.gov.tr/en

Istanbul Archaeological Museums
Address: 34122 Fatih/İstanbul
Tel: +90 212 520 7741
http://www.istanbularkeoloji.gov.tr/main_page

Pizza de Lavia
Address: Nobethane CD, Istanbul
https://www.facebook.com/pages/Pizza-De-Lavia/539457726116136

Gülhane Park
Address: Alemdar Mah. Alemdar Cad. Eminonu/Cagaloglu, Fatih, 34122, Istanbul

Gelata Tower
Address: Buyuk Hendek Cad., Istanbul

• Day 3 •

On the third day, we're sending you to bathe! Yes, you read that correctly. Here is something you simply must do at least once while in Turkey: Visit a **Turkish *hamam*** (bath). If you're a true first-timer, this can be a formidable experience, but don't fret—we've got you covered. Depending on where you chose to stay, your hotel may offer Turkish bath services. If not, we recommend <u>**Çemberlitaş Hamamı**</u>,

There are a variety of **bath options** to choose from: self-service (you bring your own soap, towel, etc., and bathe yourself), Indian head massages, aromatherapy massages, reflexology, and more, but we recommend the **Scrubbing, Bubbles and Sultan's Bath** service where you simply turn up and someone else washes and massages all your cares away! Cost is anywhere from 80-90 TL and it's expected you'll tip your attendant anywhere from 10-20%. Be sure to check out **their website** for FAQs, current services, pricing and other information.

Hamams open as early as 6:00 am and close around midnight, so the choice is yours—you can do this first thing in the morning, or before returning to your hotel after a day of spontaneity. Perhaps today you can partake of **one of the amazing tours** we recommended earlier?

For dinner, we'd love you to take a cab or bus to dine at **Pierre Loti Café**, near the Eyüp mosque. The cafe is on a hill and we recommend taking the cliff railway up and walking down. You'll see signs posted near the mosque.

They've got **great live music** and **even better steaks**. The prices are admittedly tourist-geared (though not *too* bad) but the **view of the Golden Horn area** from here is so fantastic that it makes the higher pricing well worth it in our opinion. (Ask for a table near the terrace!) Also, **bring cash**, as of now you can't pay with a credit card.

Location Information:

Çemberlitaş Hamamı
Address: Çemberlitaş Hamamı, Vezirhan Cad. No: 8, 34440, Çemberlitaş / İstanbul
Tel: +90 212 522 79 74 or +90 212 520 18 50
http://www.cemberlitashamami.com/index.php?dil=en

Pierre Loti Café
Address: Gümüşsuyu Karyağdı Sokak, Eyüp, Istanbul
Tel: +90 212 581 26 96

• Day 4 •

A visit to one or more of the **Prince Islands** (Prens Adaları in Turkish), and a boat tour on the Bosphorus should keep you pretty busy today after a quick breakfast at your hotel.

To get to any of the nine Princes' Islands, you just take one of the ferries operated by **IDO** (the fastest), or by Şehir Hatları. All the ferries depart from **Kabataş ferry docks**, which is on the European side of the Bosphorus. We suggest staying on the ferry until you reach **Heybeliada**, a charming island we think you'll really enjoy.

Getting to the Kabataş docks is simple. You can take the **T1 Bağcılar-Kabataş Tram**, or the **Kabataş-Taksim Füniküler (Funicular)**.

Şehir Hatları is Istanbul's official ferry company and they offer the best **Bosphorus tour** experience. You can choose between a long or short tour.

Check **their website** for the most current schedule and booking. http://en.sehirhatlari.com.tr/en

• Day 5 •

If this is the last day of your trip, we suggest visiting a spot you may have wanted to see in Istanbul but didn't get to due to time constraints or any other circumstances.

You can also visit the **Egyptian and Spice Bazaars.** Stroll through and enjoy being in a true Middle Eastern shopping Bazaar. Let the potent spices fill your senses; shop for **cashmere scarves, eclectic jewelry and exotic teas!** Then you can spend the remainder of the day however you'd like. Perhaps another soothing hamam? Or maybe end the day with a relaxing boat or guided tour? Or with a stroll through **Taksim Square** to people-watch the locals? There are lots of beggars and peddlers to avoid here but it's a popular meeting place for locals.

However you choose to spend day five — enjoy!

Location Information:

Egyptian Bazaar
Address: Ragip Gumuspala Cad. Eminonu/Cagaloglu, Fatih, Istanbul

Spice Bazaar
Address: Rustem Pasa Mahallesi, 34116, Istanbul

• Best Places For Travelers on a Budget •

Like most beautiful cities, Istanbul is known for being home to some of the best hotels, restaurants, bars and shops. However, if you're **on a budget**, we can point you to the accommodations and restaurants that offer the best values in Istanbul. Call or visit their websites for **current rates and availability**.

Bargain Istanbul Sleeps

Our top recommendation is **Hotellino Istanbul**. This three-star hotel is located within walking distance of most of Istanbul's main historical attractions: Haghia Sophia, The Blue Mosque, Topkapi Palace, Basilica Cistern, The Grand Bazaar and The Spice Bazaar.

Hotellino Istanbul
Address: Nöbethane Cd No:5, Sirkeci, İstanbul
Tel: +90 212 513 1212
http://www.hotellinoistanbul.com

Another very affordable two-star hotel located in the old city is **Hotel Agan**, nice and cozy and also in a great, central location!

Hotel Agan
Address: Hoca Paşa Mh., 34110, Fatih/İstanbul
Tel: +90 212 527 85 51
http://www.aganhotel.com/en

Bargain Istanbul Eats

Love a good wrap or kebab? The "wrap artists" at Istanbul's **Dürümzade** serve up chicken kebab (*tavuk şiş*), spicy minced beef (Adana kebab), or mild (Urfa kebab), in flatbread or on a plate if you prefer. All is tasty and affordable and you can even grab a salad.

Dürümzade
Address: Hüseyinağa Mh., 34435, Beyoğlu/İstanbul
Tel: +90 212 249 01 47

Looking for burgers in Istanbul? Head to **Kızılkayalar Hamburger.** The sign says *Islak Burger,* which means "wet burger" in English—best burger joint in the city. No seating, so you'll have to take it to go or dig in standing there; either way, believe us when we say it's worth it!

Kızılkayalar Hamburger
Address: Sira Selviler Cad. No:2/L | Taksim Meydanl Istiklal Girisi, Istanbul
Tel: +90 212 251 1357
http://www.kizilkayalar.com.tr/english

Here is a list of **the most inexpensive and tasty Turkish street foods** we recommend you not miss while in Istanbul:

- Köfte (Meatball)
- Mantı (Dumpling)
- Pide (Turkish pizza)
- Döner (meat dish)
- Rice Pilaf
- Lahmacun (Turkish flatbread)
- Wraps
- Tantuni (Turkish burrito)

• Best Places for Ultimate Luxury •

"And, we have no such thing as a budget anymore. Our manager freaks when we show him the bill. We're lavish to the bone..." — **Freddie Mercury**

Luxury Istanbul Sleeps

One of Istanbul's **most luxurious and divine hotels** in our experience is **Four Seasons Istanbul at the Bosphorus**. Housed in a former Ottoman palace, it's entirely possible you won't ever wish to leave. There is also a sister property in Sultanahmet, which is close to sightseeing and shopping. **So why not do both?**

Four Seasons Istanbul at the Bosphorus
Address: Yıldız Mh., Çırağan Caddesi No: 28, 34349, Beşiktaş/Istanbul
Tel: +90 212 381 4000
http://www.fourseasons.com/bosphorus

Four Seasons Istanbul at Sultanahmet
Address: Tevkifhane Sok No: 1, 34110, Sultanahmet/Istanbul
Tel: +90 212 402 3000
http://www.fourseasons.com/istanbul

Both the **Blue Mosque and the Topkapi Palace** are close to our next favorite spot for luxury in Istanbul: **DoubleTree by Hilton Istanbul - Old Town**, a very warm and friendly five-star hotel with staff members who greet you upon arrival bearing *the* most delicious chocolate chip cookies in town!

DoubleTree by Hilton Istanbul - Old Town
Address: Beyazıt Mh., Ordu Cad. No: 31, 34130 Fatih/İstanbul
Tel: +90 212 453 5800
http://doubletree3.hilton.com/en/hotels/turkey/d oubletree-by-hilton-hotel-istanbul-old-town-ISTOTDI/index.html

Luxury Istanbul Eats

For a cool Mediterranean flavor on Turkish fare, dine at **Müzedechanga**. The view is amazing, the atmosphere divine, the food scrumptiously delicious!

Müzedechanga
Address: Emirgan Mh., Sakıp Sabancı Cd No: 22, İstanbul
Tel: +90 212 323 0901
http://www.changa-istanbul.com/v2/muzedechangamain-tr.asp

Our next favorite **upscale restaurant** in Istanbul is the extravagant **Borsa Restaurant**. Beautifully stylish design, and the food is fabulous! They're **open late** 7 days a week.

Borsa Restaurant
Address: Lütfi Kırdar Uluslararası Kongre ve Sergi
Sarayı, Istanbul
Tel: +90 212 2324201
http://www.borsaselfservis.com

• Istanbul Nightlife •

Great Bars in Istanbul

If you're the **bar type** and you're looking for the best ones in town to hang out and have drink, we've hand-picked **the cream of the crop** for you right here!

For some of the most **original cocktails** in town, check out **360 Istanbul**—and be not surprised if you run into **a celebrity or two** while you're in there.

360 Istanbul
Address: Istiklal Street, Mısır Apartment, 8th Floor
No: 163 Beyoglu, Istanbul
Tel: +90 212 251 1042
http://www.360istanbul.com/eng

Urban Cafe Beyoğlu is a low-key café-bar with good vibes. It's all about the simplicity and provides a great opportunity for some nice bonding time with your travel friends or family.

Urban Cafe Beyoğlu
Address: Kartal Sok. No: 6/A Galatasaray, Beyoglu, Istanbul
 Tel: +90 212 252 1325
http://www.urbanbeyoglu.com

Great Clubs in Istanbul

For an enjoyable night out (you may even wish to let loose and go a bit wild in Istanbul!), one of the following nightclubs should do the trick. Go on, get out there — dance, party and meet some new people!

Indigo Istanbul
Address: Tomtom Mh., Istiklal Cd., Akarsu Sk No: 1-2-4-5, 34433, Beyoğlu/Istanbul
Tel: 90 212 244 8567
http://indigo-istanbul.com

Reina
Address: Muallim Naci Cad. No: 44 | Ortakoy, Besiktas, 34347, Istanbul
Tel: +90 212 259 5919
http://www.reina.com.tr/en

Great Music and Dance

The four major styles of dance in Istanbul are: **Bar**, **Halay**, **Horon** and **Zeybek**. Turkish dance is **incredibly exotic**. We highly recommend visiting **Sultana's 1001 Nights Show** to experience it for yourself! You can even enjoy a tasty bite while taking in the belly dance.

Sultana's
Address: Cumhuriyet Caddesi 16/1, Elmadağ, Elmadağ, Istanbul
Tel: +90 212 219 3904
http://www.sultanas-nights.com

Great Live Music in Istanbul

Turkish music is basically a mix of various influences: Central Asian folk music, Arabic, Byzantine, Greek, Ottoman, Persian, Armenian, and Balkan music.

Munzur Cafe Bar features great live performances of traditional Turkish music.
Address: Katip Çelebi Mh., 34433, Beyoğlu/Istanbul
Tel: +90 212 245 4669
http://www.munzurcafebar.com/munzur

Hayal *Kahvesi* is another very popular spot in Istanbul for entertaining live performances. Turkish artists play here regularly so check the website for the latest bookings.

Hayal *Kahvesi*
Address: Burunbahce Mevki Agaclik Mesire Yeri
Cubuklu Cad. No: 18 | Cubuklu, Beykoz, Istanbul
Tel: +90 212 413 6880
http://www.hayalkahvesi.com.tr

Great Theatre in Istanbul

Watching a Turkish play can really open your eyes
to the sheer richness of Turkish culture. If you love
the theater or just appreciate wonderful entertainment,
take in a show at the **Galata Perform** performing arts
theater. Talented **Turkish artists** write and produce
some amazing works you can enjoy during your stay.
Check out their website for current events and show-
times.

Galata Perform
Address: Bereketzade Mh., Büyük Hendek Cd No:21,
30040 İstanbul
Tel: +90 212 243 9991
http://eng.galataperform.com

• Conclusion •

We hope that our guide to **the eclectic city of Istanbul** most helpful as you plan for your trip. We've done our part, now it's your turn to go, see and enjoy **this wonderful Eurasian city**. We wish you a **very safe and fun-filled trip** to Turkey!

Our most warm regards,

The Passport to European Travel Guides Team

Visit our Blog! Grab more of our signature guides for all your travel needs!

http://www.passporttoeuropeantravelguides.blogspot.com

★ **Join our mailing list** ★ to follow our Travel Guide Series. You'll be automatically entered for a chance to win a **$100 Visa Gift Card** in our monthly drawings! Be sure to respond to the confirmation e-mail to complete the subscription.

• About the Authors •

Passport to European Travel Guides is an eclectic team of international jet setters who know exactly what travelers and tourists want in a cut-to-the-chase, comprehensive travel guide that suits a wide range of budgets.

Our growing collection of distinguished European travel guides are guaranteed to give first-hand insight to each locale, complete with day-to-day, guided itineraries you won't want to miss!

We want our brand to be your official Passport to European Travel — one you can always count on!

Bon Voyage!

The Passport to European Travel Guides Team
http://www.passporttoeuropeantravelguides.blogspot.com

Printed in the USA
CPSIA information can be obtained
at www.ICGtesting.com
LVHW012233010224
770720LV00007B/343

9 781519 149176